Teaching in Perspective

Teaching in Perspective

AVIS McMULLEN

Teaching in Perspective

by Avis McMullen

© 2000, Word Aflame Press
Hazelwood, MO 63042-2299

Cover Design by Paul Povolni

Cover Art by Elizabeth Swisher

All Scripture quotations in this book are from the King James Version of the Bible unless otherwise identified.

All rights reserved. No portion of this publication may be reproduced, stored in an electronic system, or transmitted in any form or by any means, electronic, mechanical, photocopy, recording, or otherwise, without the prior permission of Word Aflame Press. Brief quotations may be used in literary reviews.

Printed in United States of America

Printed by

Library of Congress Cataloging-in-Publication Data

McMullen, Avis.
    Teaching in perspective / Avis McMullen.
        p.   cm.
    Includes bibliographical references (p.).
    ISBN 1–56722–246–3
    I. Teaching.   2. Classroom management.   I. Title.
    LB1025.3 .M39   2000
    371.102—dc21

                                                                       00-035927

Contents

1. Physical, Cognitive, and Social Development..... 9
2. Setting Up a Learning Environment 21
3. Sweet Pickle Relish, Sunflowers, and Old Spare Tires........................ 35
4. Reach, Teach, Evaluate (The Plan) 49
5. Classroom Discipline....................... 59
6. Just Legal Matters 73
7. Wit, Wisdom, and Whatnots................. 81

chapter one

Physical, Cognitive, and Social Development

"Now today, boys and girls, we are going to fill your itty-bitty hearts with all you need to know about how to apply for a job successfully. So, I need all of you to come to the story circle and sit on your name tag," cooed the teacher to her adolescent students.

The first response in my mind is, "Totally inappropriate!" One should never address teenagers as a nursery class or ever expect the nursery to respond to, "All right, it is time to continue with the procedures that we began yesterday in class." Like wearing a fur coat while swimming, such behavior is extremely out of place.

As children grow, they progress through many stages. Every child must, in some way, pass along the same path of development. On this journey there will be many changes physically, mentally, psychologically, and socially. We will endeavor to discuss these changes in the basic patterns of development. The ages may not be exact, but the order usually is. Some children learn faster in certain stages, yet they may be slower in others. Each child is unique and develops at his own pace.

Both genetic makeup and environment influence a child's development. Have you ever wondered why some children act, look, and think so much like Grandpa, Auntie, or some other relative whom they see very little of? The genes are our first gift; we have no control over them. However, the second influence is one that we can do much about. The environment in which children are brought up will determine how prepared they are to face the adult world. The following composition describes the influence of adults in the life of a child.

Children Learn What They Live

If a child lives with criticism, he learns to condemn.
If a child lives with hostility, he learns to fight.
If a child lives with ridicule, he learns to be shy.
If a child lives with shame, he learns to feel guilty.
If a child lives with tolerance, he learns to be patient.
If a child lives with encouragement, he learns confidence.
If a child lives with praise, he learns to appreciate.
If a child lives with fairness, he learns justice.
If a child lives with security, he learns to have a family.
If a child lives with approval, he learns to like himself.
If a child lives with acceptance and friendship,
   he learns to find love in the world.
—Dorthy Law Nolte

Physical, Cognitive, and Social Development

There is very little difference in a baby girl and a baby boy other than the obvious physical difference. They both need the same amount of love, food, water, and shelter.

The infant-to-toddler stage is what Jean Piaget called the *sensorimotor period* (zero to two years). During this period, children will progress more than at any other time in their lives. In two short years they will move from total helplessness to primitive independence.

The beginning of development comes from reflex, such as sucking and flailing. Within weeks there is a conscious effort to bring the fist to the mouth and suck, roll over, and make cooing sounds. There is a more definite awareness of surroundings, for now children can focus their eyes and follow movement as well as respond to voices. At approximately three months, the first voluntary smiles become evident, and simple chuckles soon follow.

Around this time, babies may be able to sit propped on a pillow for short periods of times, and they will make more efforts to reach and grasp. Development speeds along so rapidly now that every day is a new world with more to conquer. Soon they can sit alone and crawl.

At the same time, language is developing. The mother will soon learn the cries of hunger, pain, restlessness, fright, and other feelings that the baby expresses. Syllables are formed and take on meaning.

When children are about one year old, they can speak in short phrases and may begin taking their first steps. The following year is a year of mastering these skills. There is not a place that they will not explore or a sound that they will not make. All of these activities are developing the mind and body for the coming years when walking and talking will no longer take conscious effort. Toilet

TEACHING IN PERSPECTIVE

training, dressing, and feeding skills will develop by the end of the second year.

Cognitive, or mental, development also occurs rapidly. During the first two years of life the child develops the ability to differentiate between self and objects and between self and others. A supportive environment is vital for cognitive and emotional development. Of course, the basic needs should be met with plenty of nurturing, but providing plenty of games and toys is important. Interactive play is a must for every baby.

Psychoanalyst Erik Erikson has outlined the crises in psychosocial development. At each stage there are certain developments of social awareness and emotions that contribute to our personalities. During the first year of life a baby's psychosocial crisis is *basic trust versus basic mistrust*. Children will be trusting if they have found rewarding reactions from the people and things in their environment, but mistrust comes from negative feedback or responses to their interactions.

In the second year of life, children face *autonomy versus shame and doubt*. Children who are becoming toilet trained, starting to dress and feed themselves, and learning limitations for protection against their own impulses will develop a positive sense of self-control (autonomy) and personal pride with proper guidance. Failure in this guidance will bring a sense of shame and compulsive doubt of themselves and others.

On a last note about the sensorimotor period, toddlers need repetition to learn because they have short attention spans and are short-term learners. They may throw a toy on the floor fifty times for someone to pick up, but in doing so they master a skill and muscle coordination that

Physical, Cognitive, and Social Development

they will need later. This also explains the nursery rhymes, counting songs, silly rhyming songs, and funny sounding words that they want to hear over and over and over.

I believe Weylen, my second son, began to make conversation with this first phrase: "'Gin, Mama." So here I went 'gin, singing "Old MacDonald," "The Farmer in the Dell," "Knick-Knack-Paddy-Whack," and on and on and on for miles and miles down the road as we traveled in the car.

The *preoperational period* (two to seven years), Piaget's second stage of development, brings to light more differences in the sexes. Their environment usually demands differences, and they began role playing. Girls often mature faster than boys for the next several years. We often see greater coordination in girls than in boys of the same age.

While the changes may not be as radical as before, they are still great in this period of development. The physical changes and growth allow children to run faster, go farther, and express themselves clearer. They will learn to ride a bike, play games, swing, slide, climb, and much more. Short sentences will develop into full conversations and expressive dialogue. It is common to see a child this age using great imagination and pretending.

One day, while I was folding the laundry, three-year-old Tyrel, my first son, took a rope belt of mine and tied it between the cabinet and the dryer door. He then began to repeat, "Dis jail. I Pah. You Silas." It took a while for me to figure out that we were in prison and that he was Paul and I was Silas. After insisting that we sing, he let us out of jail. It dawned on me that the last Sunday school lesson had been about the deliverance of Paul and Silas.

The cognitive development in this stage will have a

couple of perceptive limitations. *Centration* is one limitation and is characterized by being able to focus only on one dimension of a situation at a time. It is hard for children of this age to understand size and number in relation to the situation. For instance, they may insist that a tall, thin glass holds more water than a short, wide glass because the level of water is higher.

Another limitation is that their thought is *irreversible*. They cannot comprehend that an object can change and then return to its original state, such as changing a ball of Play-Doh into a snake and then back into a ball. They understand the ball, snake, and ball, but not the process between.

Aside from these limitations, however, children learn skills and information quickly and eagerly. They focus on success instead of failure. The pleasure of an activity is enough to encourage the behavior. Their new physical and mental strength encourages ambitions that may lead them beyond boundaries of their ability or be forbidden by parents.

Adult guidance in accepting these boundaries and coming to terms with them is important in Erikson's psychosocial crisis of this stage, *initiative versus guilt*. Adults in the environment can encourage or destroy the healthy curiosity that is built into every child. If children are not able to come to terms with the set boundaries, they may be troubled with guilt.

If nurtured during the formative stages, a child's sense of humor can be a great asset in coping later in life. During this stage the pre-educational skills are extremely important, and learning them should be made fun.

New words and actions are exciting to a child but can

Physical, Cognitive, and Social Development

be a source of embarrassment to parents. I remember a few things that I did as a little girl and wonder at how my mother put up with me. One day, while in line at a church camp meeting, I had a clothespin in my hand. Evidently, I had only recently become familiar with grasshoppers, because after clipping the clothespin to a total stranger's dress hem, I shouted, "Look, Mama! My grasshopper is biting that lady!" Mother wanted to disappear.

I will never forget when my kindergarten teacher began teaching words like migration, vibration, and hibernation. I cracked the family up by announcing, "Look! Those birds are vibrating south."

The least noticeable physical change occurs during the *period of concrete operations* (seven to eleven years). The greatest change of this time in the life of children is at the cognitive level. The limitations that once held them back are now reversed and become accomplishments.

At this point of *decentration*, they have the ability to shift their attention from one part of a situation to another. They can understand that the same amount of water is in both the tall and short glass. They also comprehend that twelve beans are still twelve beans whether placed in a circle, row, or heap. By the end of this stage children may even be able to grasp the transformation that occurs when sugar is dissolved in water.

Their thinking is now *reversible*. They can realize that one action is a direct result of a previous action or set of actions.

By building on the trust, autonomy, and initiative that they developed earlier, children in this stage can achieve a sense of industry. They spend the first years of school learning the mechanics of letters and numbers. Mastering the three R's (reading, 'riting, and 'rithmetic) and developing a working knowledge of the basic application of these skills will prepare them for the rest of their education and for life.

I once heard a wise teacher say, "In kindergarten through third grade kids learn to read, but from fourth grade on they read to learn." This statement is exactly in line with the developmental stages. Children now have the endurance to stick with a job until it is completed. They will strive to perform according to their and others' expectations. If they are unable to perform a necessary task acceptably, there is a danger of them developing a sense of inferiority, and this prevents future trying. For this reason, parents and teachers need to offer a great deal of positive reinforcement for attempting a task as well as completing it. Erikson defines this psychosocial crisis as *industry versus inferiority*.

Often during this stage, personality problems arise and learning disorders are discovered. The diversity among children becomes apparent as their education progresses. This should be a time in life that has boundaries wide enough to allow maximum growth and narrow enough to maintain safety and respect.

One illustration is to compare a child to a bar of soap. If you do not hold tightly enough to the soap, it will slip into the water in danger of being lost forever, but if you hold too tightly it will shoot out of your hand and disappear into the same water with the same dangers. A child is to be guided gently but firmly through these formative years—protected yet allowed to take chances.

The *period of formal operations* (eleven years through adulthood) is the final stage of cognitive devel-

Physical, Cognitive, and Social Development

opment that Piaget identified. In adolescence the child reaches sexual maturity. Girls are still slightly ahead of boys until about twenty-five years of age. Children usually reach their full height at around sixteen.

The teen years have proven to be a mystery and the most feared time for parents and children. However, understanding the cognitive development can shed some light on the whole picture. Children can now make hypotheses and draw conclusions that are not obvious. When shown a picture of a crying girl, for instance, they no longer just respond that she is sad. Teens can suggest reasons for the crying, such as death of relative, pain, anger, and then discuss causes for the reasons.

Teens have an acute sense of growth, aging, and death. There is often a strong opinion about world affairs such as hunger, homelessness, peace, and justice. During this final stage, abstract thinking becomes prevalent, and they may participate in confrontations with elaborate arguments that support their opinions. Boundaries must be widened yet maintained.

Scores on tests that measure high-level mental processes, such as mathematics and analogies, peak in late adolescence. Scores on tests that measure the amount of knowledge, however, improve with age.

This is a time of questioning and challenging, as the establishing of identity takes place. Erikson identified two psychosocial development crises for this stage. First is *identity versus role confusion*—a time in which teens establish their identity. If they are unsatisfied with themselves, then they will struggle with role confusion and may become committed to some fashionable hero or ideal. The second crisis, *intimacy versus isolation*, occurs during the years of young adulthood.

There are two more stages of life that we will mention briefly. The period of middle age or the "prime of life" is a time when the psychosocial crisis is *generativity versus stagnation*. The last phase of life, old age, brings *ego integrity versus despair*. Knowing about these adult phases helps make us aware of the needs of people who surround us in our lives daily. The adults in our society are the role models for our children. When we have healthy, well-rounded adults, we can train healthy, well-rounded children.

Each stage builds upon the stage before. My father was a carpenter. When he built a house, he started at the foundation. He added the walls only after he felt secure in the strength of the floor. The roof could only be in place when the walls would support it. So the development of a child goes step by step from birth to death. No child is like any other. Each one is an individual. Yet, there are some patterns and generalities that can guide us along as we establish the best environment possible for every child we influence.

I'm Only Me

I'm only me,
The best me I can be.
I'm different, it is true,
In what I think, feel, or do.

My heart, my soul, my mind—
All unique, one of a kind;
But in my own special way
I'll be me—my best me today!
—Avis McMullen

chapter two

Setting Up a Learning Environment

When children feel comfortable with their environment they will explore and learn voluntarily. This is true at every level of development. It is the responsibility of the instructor to set up an environment that provides balance in play and work, in guidance and experimenting, in structure and freedom of expression. The days of "Come in, sit down, be quiet, and learn" have passed; modern technology competes for the attention of our students.

Setting up an educational classroom involves many factors. The primary factor to consider is the age and development of the audience.

TEACHING IN PERSPECTIVE

Play Today?

You say you love your children
And are concerned they learn today?
So am I—that's why I'm providing
A variety of kinds of play.

You're asking me the value
Of blocks and other such play.
Your children are solving problems;
They will use that skill every day.

You're asking what is the value
Of having your children play.
Your daughter's creating a tower;
She may be a builder someday.

You're saying you don't want your son
To play in that "sissy" way!
He's learning to cuddle a doll;
He may be a father someday.

You're questioning the interest centers;
They just look like useless play.
Your children are making choices;
They'll be on their own someday.

You're worried your children aren't learning,
And later they'll have to pay.
They're learning patterns for learning,
For they'll be learners always.

—Author Unknown

Setting Up a Learning Environment

We cannot expect children to go swimming in fur coats. Teens would not learn to be teens in a classroom designed for five-year-olds, nor would toddlers thrive in a class for older children. We must make it comfortable for students and teacher to interact.

Just as no two students are alike, no two teachers are alike. Therefore, the following guidelines are not etched in stone as the one and only way. Use what fits you, develop your own technique, learn from watching and listening to others, and then enjoy teaching.

Some teachers work better with everything out where they can see it and get to it easily. Others need tidy rooms with everything put away. Some can handle more noise than the one next door. Brightness may suit one and duller colors someone else. Each classroom must be set up to reflect the teacher's own personality.

If you are someone who needs to rearrange after every rain cloud, get lightweight furniture. If you are happy in your room, you are more apt to meet the needs of the children, and they will be happy there, too. I have caught myself hanging out in Mrs. Crowson's third-grade classroom at work, because it feels like Grandma's house. She has ruffles and pillows with gingham cloths and animal pictures decorating every area. Her personality is so well reflected in the room that it may surprise you to find out that she is still in her thirties. She is soft spoken yet firm, sweet as honey, and pretty as a peach.

Here are some basic guidelines to set up a classroom physically. First, make sure that the furniture is suitable for the size of the children. You will need larger furniture for some students and smaller for others, even within the same age and developmental stage.

Second, have visuals and materials at eye level for the children who will be using them.

Third, if they are not supposed to touch something, do not put it where they can reach it without supervision! Setting up a teacher-only area is a good idea, for it teaches respect for others, but it is not a guarantee that some little fingers will not go wandering.

Finally, keep the environment safe. Be aware of sharp objects at all levels. Consider paths within the room and keep them clear. When there is a lot of active involvement, make sure that there is plenty of room to move without bumping others. There will be unavoidable accidents no matter how much you plan, but you can cut down on their severity by thinking ahead.

In the spring of 1985 before my youngest son was born in the summer, I was tired, very pregnant, and about as graceful as a hippo in a slick bathtub. The kindergartners were working at their tables while I came around for individual assistance. The early childhood class had also

Setting Up a Learning Environment

come in with this class for art. As I stood and turned to go to the next table, one of the little three-year-olds came to show me his picture. Not seeing him but sensing him and already having my body in motion, I tried to stop but lost my balance and wound up on my feet and hands over this child's head with my posterior straight up in the air. I could not get up or down until the boy got down on his hands and knees and crawled out from under me. Then I lowered myself to the floor and had to sit there until I quit laughing. All of the children and the early childhood teacher laughed when they found out that I was okay. Thank goodness, I had planned wide aisles between the tables.

The tools of education need to be appropriate to the children's developmental stage. We must keep in mind the characteristics of children at their different levels and remember that each progression builds on previous experiences. The more experiences, the stronger the structure.

The traditional school setting has approximately two to three age levels. However, almost any other situation that children will be involved in includes a wider age range. Some of these situations may be Sunday school, vacation Bible school, summer camp, playing in the neighborhood, and parties. With this in mind, let us consider four age groups. Again, we should note that these recommendations are generalities and must be made to fit each individual situation.

The classroom for children from *birth to two years* is often called the nursery. The furniture needs to include baby beds, highchairs, playpens, walkers, strollers, play mats, diaper-changing tables and baby-safe toys. Rattlers, squeakers, pull-along toys, push toys, cloth books, plastic blocks, and any other easy-to-clean, baby-safe toys are welcome. The room should be set up with quiet times or areas for sleeping babies. The teacher must provide ample space for the toys that require a lot of movement.

During this stage, children need exuberant, positive reinforcement. The early stages of language are developing, so talk to them about everything, whether you think they can understand or not. Sit in an armchair and hold them in your lap while you read to them. Remember, each child is different. Some may like to be cuddled, while others may want their space.

Classrooms for *toddlers to kindergarten age* should include miniature furniture. The toys and tools should include puzzles, blocks of different sizes and shapes, dolls and home furnishings, dress-up items, children's easy books, and if possible a computer or electronic game with educational purpose. They should now be encouraged to learn pre-mathematics and pre-reading skills. This will involve problem solving, constructing, manipulating, counting, singing, and reciting. It is extremely important to read aloud to them as often as possible. Many of them may be able to count to twenty, say the alphabet, and print their name. (Just a note from kindergarten teachers: Teach them to write their name with a capital first and the rest in lower-case letters.)

There is a natural wonder as their little minds are still thinking in the concrete stage. I am often faced with the wide-eyed, wondering question, "Wow! How did you do that?" as I teach art. I usually tell them, "I'm magic, so call me Ms. Magic. You can be magic too. Here, I'll throw you some of my magic." Then with a sweep of my arm I pretend to throw magic over the room. When they see that

Setting Up a Learning Environment

they can do the same art with their materials they shout, "Hey, Ms. Magic, I'm magic, too!"

By the end of kindergarten they will amaze you at the knowledge that they possess. Children learn to play by watching the adults in their environment. They will establish lifelong patterns of feelings, social skills, behavior, and learning by the time they are five years old.

Again, each child is different and must be allowed to be different. Comparing one child's behavior to another's is not wise.

The attention span is still very short, and activities should vary often. Structure, such as circle-time explanations and guided practice teaching, should be brief and to the point.

Reinforcing good behavior will often get better results than punishing negative actions. (See chapter 5.) If children are allowed to solve simple social situations, they seem to forgive much sooner than if adults interfere.

Preschool children grow and change rapidly. We should allow their personalities to develop without making them become mirrors of what we want them to be. Teaching is guidance, not creation.

The environment for children entering *the stage of concrete operations* and leaving the preoperational stage will need transformations in many ways. As children move from informal to formal education, the tools change with them. Now books with less pictures and more words replace the pre-primers. Learning to play formal games with definite rules and guidelines is necessary to the development of social skills as well as problem-solving strategies.

I can remember trying to figure out where to stand in my third-grade class so I would be chosen when the leader of the game started saying, "Eeny meeny miny mo." It forced me to think of odd and even numbers, ordinal numbers, and syllabication, and I had to do it fast. Errors in my judgment sent my mind into rewind, and I would not stop until I figured out why I was missed. That is when I learned that some kids said, "Blue shoe, blue shoe," while others said, "Nine horses in a fence." That was quite a startling revelation!

Attention spans increase with age. However, the attention span is only as long as the interest. I do not have a very long endurance when I am forced to listen to sports and scores, but when someone starts talking about the wonders of animals and nature I will sit all day long. Know your audience and their interests. Make an effort to find out what their hobbies are and what they like. You can do surveys, interviews, artwork, and much more to gain this information.

Have visuals at eye level, and arrange furniture to provide minimal disruptions. Are the paths accessible and adequate for movement? Are the children permitted to have access to things that are readily available to them? Are the items you want them to have access to readily available? Does the arrangement promote disruptive behavior, or is it conducive to learning?

Small-group activities and projects are an excellent way to promote social development. Peer interaction can be one of the best tools for maintaining class control. The classroom should be child friendly with visual prompts, appropriate furniture, and an abundance of activities that reinforce the skills being taught.

By the end of elementary school, children have a good sense of space and where they are. They know that they

Setting Up a Learning Environment

live in a neighborhood, in a town, in a county, in a state, in a country, on a continent, on the planet earth within the universe. They also are very aware of life and death, family, friends, and relationships with others. Emotions such as love, trust, inferiority, and acceptance are gaining importance. You can make or break a child's fragile self-esteem by the way you react to him or her.

As I went into the fourth grade, my little brother was five months old. (I had been the baby for nine and a half years.) My big sister was in junior high school, so Mother was having to deal with an adolescent and a baby. My third-grade teacher had put a love to read in me as well as an eagerness to achieve and succeed. And I had one fault that my fourth-grade teacher could not see past: I talked to my friends in class. Every day she would put my name on the board and place checks behind it until the end of the day. Just before the bell rang she would take out her little paddle and march all those with checks to the front of the room for one lick per check. On several occasions, I got ten licks while holding onto the chalk rail in front of my friends, and with every lick I thought that someday I would do something to get her back.

At first I tried to comply with her rules, but after I received a few undeserved checks, I quit caring. I also quit caring about my work, my grades, my family, and life itself. My grades dropped from A's and B's in third grade to low C's, D's, and F's in fourth grade.

I was promoted to fifth grade, but in spite of a wonderful teacher, I continued to go downhill. This downward spiral continued until the ninth grade, when a teacher cared enough to fail me in English, and I had to go to summer school. While sitting in summer English class I decided that the only one who could help me was me, and I began to climb out of the hole that had me trapped. In the tenth grade my grades went back to A's and B's.

I also realized that my social life was horrible. I was aggressive and would beat up anybody who looked at me wrong. I made a commitment to God, and my family moved across Texas to start a home missions work in Alpine. My life took an about-face. I realized that the best way to get back at that fourth-grade teacher who did not take time to see a child with major troubles and great potential was to become a caring, loving teacher myself, and thus, a dream was born.

The junior high years bring *the stage of formal operations*. Classrooms need to be equipped with furniture that reflects the modern trends. Antiquated furnishing can be repainted, made over, and rearranged with effort and little cost. It is not difficult to make teens' environment a comfortable place to be without losing structure. The students often like to be a part of the transition. This brings about a sense of belonging and ownership that can cut down on distractions and disruptions.

All visuals and decorations are now pretty much at the teacher's eye level. There may be a great difference in the sizes of the students, however. The teacher must make sure that there is ample space for every student.

Teens are territorial and possessive, often assuming positions as in a pecking order. Flaring tempters, budding courtships, and general horseplay are a few of the challenges to the organized classroom.

They often have great concern for world affairs and current events. It is easy to rally a group to discuss the pros and cons of cutting timber in the Amazon rain for-

Setting Up a Learning Environment

est. They will talk about divorce and its effect on America, but they may not be ready to discuss divorce in their homes.

It is important not to humiliate or embarrass teens in front of their peers if at all possible. It is better to sacrifice yourself than to inflict lasting hurt to a child.

I recently had a situation in which I had to make a choice between a teen and myself. I was a dorm matron at a church camp for ages twelve to fourteen. I chose a bunk bed on the bottom at the back of the dorm. While I was helping the other girls make beds and set up camp, a child chose the bunk over my bed. After everyone was settled, I found out that she was a bed wetter. My first thought was to move or make her move, but if I did, then all of her new-found friends would know. I also found out that she was a foster child recently removed from a very dysfunctional family. If I moved either one of us, everyone would find out why, so I simply decided to get up, wash sheets, and bathe if she had an accident.

I secretly reminded her every night to take her medicine. Everything was fine until the last night, when we both forgot the medication. She wet the bed. As I started to wake her the next morning, she was almost in tears and whispered her plight to me. So I said, "Hurry, go take a shower. I'll take your sheets and pack them to go home and no one will know." And no one did. My reaction to her dilemma made it less stressful.

As older teens make the final move from child to adult, the teacher must be ready to answer career and life-planning questions without inflicting judgment or producing robots. It is very important to allow each one to remain an individual. They need role models, but we do not want carbon copies. There is a delicate balance here in education and socialization.

The room should reflect the personalities of the teacher and the students. There is currently a trend toward informal settings in which there are sofas and armchairs instead of straight-back chairs and long or oval tables instead of desks. Posters and visuals should be direct and to the point. Humor is important for portraying issues in a nonthreatening way.

Money, marriage, education, career, and fitting into the adult world are all subjects of great importance to teens. Treating them with respect is a key to success in the classroom. Everyone has an opinion, and the best teachers are those who allow students to differ from them without either side losing respect for the other.

Teens often become bogged down in the details of life and find it hard to see the end. I shall never forget going in to talk to the head of the Education Department at Sul Ross State University. I told him that I needed to drop a class because of this, that, and the other. (I gave him a whole list of reasons.) He replied, "Avis, what of this will matter when you are eighty years old and in a rocking chair?" With this prompt I was able to put everything in perspective and make a rational decision that I did not regret.

chapter three

Sweet Pickle Relish, Sunflowers, and Old Spare Tires

While rummaging through discarded books from the school library, I happened upon a book by Eva Knox Evans entitled *All About Us*. This wonderful book, copyrighted in 1947, is a children's book that faces the issue of prejudice in a straightforward way. I have read it to my students and helped them to realize the individuality of everyone. One of my favorite quotes from the book is: "People are special because they are us." This sounds rather silly until we think about it in depth. Would this place be special without you and me? Maybe so, but I am not willing to find out. Here are some additional excerpts from Evans's book:

- Wouldn't it be silly if we all looked alike?
- We would get into a lot of trouble if we all looked alike!
- Wouldn't it be silly if we liked everybody in exactly the same way?
- It is very lucky that we don't all like exactly the same kind of people. But have you ever stopped to think about how you select your friends?
- Do you choose your friends because of the way they look? You may not, but many do. They sometimes choose a special someone for a friend only because he looks a certain way.

As we enter the classroom, do we see colors, sizes, and developmental stages, or do we see individual children with individual personalities and situations?

One of the most influential differences in the classroom is that of learning rate. There are few situations in life where everyone has equal I.Q. levels, especially in a classroom. However, we should be very cautious about labeling children. We should never set up fences and lock children into situations without giving them a chance of escape.

Often we label children in a well-intentioned effort to meet the needs of individuals. We say a child is gifted because he excels in an academic area, but what about the child who is like my neighbor—severely mentally handicapped and unable to talk but able to work two-thousand-piece puzzles in record time? Is he not gifted? Then why is he placed in a category where he can never use his gift but must constantly struggle to attain the "normal" standard?

Every person is gifted in some area, and everyone is a reluctant learner, if not learning disabled, in other areas. My poor father spent endless hours with me and a bass guitar in my hands attempting to teach me a song, any song, "Mary Had a Little Lamb," "Twinkle, Twinkle, Little Star," *anything*, but to no avail. After the umpteenth time I asked, "How do you know when to change your hands?" He finally had to admit that when it came to music I was brain-dead or rather ear-dead.

In my own two sons, I have a very accomplished reader who takes the language arts in stride but struggles painfully with mathematics, while the other one is mathematical and a true problem solver but would rather do anything than read or write. However, they are both athletic and musically inclined. I cannot say what makes them strong in certain areas while remaining weak in others.

In short, no two people are alike, and therefore no etched-in-stone prescription can be written to solve every child's needs. We must look at ways to meet every learner's need.

First of all, know your students! Know their strong points, likes, dislikes, and weaknesses. Focus on the strengths while guiding them to develop the weak areas. Allow the strengths of peers to be steppingstones for each other.

For example, I had a third-grade boy I will call Steve who was in the "special education" class. I refused to treat him any different from my "gifted" students while he was in my class. In choosing classroom groups, I made sure that each one had an academically strong student, a weak student, and a couple of average students. The children drew for job assignments and Steve drew "group leader." He took charge and made sure everyone was doing his job and doing it right. He blossomed! The group under his leading made the best papier-mâché globe of the whole class. He made the others take off paper that did not suit him; they had to redo it because he was the leader.

Steve apparently got a jump-start from that experience, because he went on to get a trophy for reading one hundred books, his reading level increased drastically, and he was promoted to fourth grade without modification to his grades. He needed to know that he could achieve and that somebody had confidence in him. As this example shows, we cannot stress too much the importance of letting each child develop to his full potential while under our influence.

The story of a little first-grade girl is not so good. I share it only to show how unjust ignorance can be. She came to me from kindergarten reading on a second- or third-grade level. She could accomplish with great success anything that I had in my classroom, which I had carefully set up to meet my children's needs on a first-grade level. I made her read pre-primers and primers and do simple adding and subtracting. She would read every book in the Library Center and ask for more. But I am sorry to say, I told myself that she needed to stay with her group and not go so far ahead because it would only cause problems.

I look back and wish a million times that I had challenged her instead of boring her out of her mind. It is true that she suffered socially due to her great hunger for knowledge, but why did I let her slip by and waste a year of teaching? I cannot answer that, but she went on to graduate with honors and become extremely successful in spite of me. I have learned that the textbook is not the solution to every need.

Another differentiating factor is *learning style*. Within a classroom, there will be multiple learning styles. Often a child will have different learning styles in different areas. We will briefly discuss three ways of looking at learning style.

We will proceed on the basis that there are really no bad learners, stupid learners, or even ridiculous or silly learners. Just as God made His children to look different on the outside, so He made them different in their brains, too.

The first difference in learning style that we will discuss is *right-brain thinking versus left-brain thinking*. The following chart describes the characteristic thought processes in each half of the brain.

Right Hemisphere	**Left Hemisphere**
Irrational	Rational
Illogical	Logical
Holistic	Linear
Spontaneous	Sequential
Feelings	Facts
Imagination	Knowledge
Art, music, mime, dance, theater	Language, math, law
Intuition	Systems, rules
Spatial	Symbolic
People-oriented	Fact-oriented
"Let's do it!"	"Let's plan first!"
Creativity	Implementation

TEACHING IN PERSPECTIVE

Right Hemisphere *(continued)*	**Left Hemisphere** *(continued)*
Think in pictures	Think in words and figures
Dreamer, playful	Worker, serious
3-D thinker	2-D thinker

"Go and make some lemonade for our guest," the mother instructed her daughters. Both went to grant the request. When Lucy Left-brain returned, she had a full pitcher of ice-cold refreshment that tasted wonderful. However, when Reba Right-brain returned, everyone was impressed at the sight, because the drink was served from a punch bowl with little sailboats floating in it among small icebergs. As everyone was served a glass, Reba realized that she had put in only half the necessary sugar, because she had doubled the recipe.

This story is humorous but close to reality. Some friends of mine think so much that they scare me. They plan, recite facts, and know so many details about so many things. Why, they go to the grocery store and only get what they went for, *and* they remember everything without a list! Then here I am. I cannot remember which way I am going. But I can weave, draw, sculpt, write, build, decorate, paint, do many crafts, work puzzles, and be creative. The half-sweet lemonade would have been mine, because I focus on impressing with creativity.

Likewise, some children with left-brain dominance will just serve good lemonade. They excel on tests and enjoy giving data back to the teacher. They are the planners and researchers of the group. They may have difficulty thinking abstract thoughts and coming up with new ideas. They may sometimes be too anxious and serious.

Then there are the predominantly right-brain thinkers who serve fantastic-looking lemonade. They are the doers and creators of the group. But trouble may come when they need to return information exactly as they received it. Keeping things in order and staying on track can be real challenges for them.

The ideal is for a person to have whole-brain dominance, drawing equally on all the characteristics we have discussed. More often, however, a person is a whole-brain thinker but has right- or left-brain dominance. My own two children and I took a survey and discovered that while I am definitely a right-brain thinker, both of my sons are whole-brain thinkers with right-brain dominance. Therefore I rely on them to help me with numbers, names, and details. We can learn to utilize a child's strong points and focus there, while attempting to strengthen the weak areas.

A second approach to learning styles is to identify three methods of learning based on the senses: *visual, auditory, and tactile*. It is important to know the strongest learning style of each child and then teach using multiple senses so that each can learn easily.

Auditory learners learn best through the sense of hearing—listening to lectures, tapes, and conversation and interacting verbally. An auditory child will understand division with remainders when the teacher explains that all numbers cannot be divided evenly and thus often there will be a remaining amount.

Visual learners learn best through sight. They need to see everything, so for them the teacher should use maps, charts, films, flashcards, chalkboards, and pictures. The visual learner will not grasp division with remainders until the teachers works a problem on the board and shows that there is a number left at the bottom.

Tactile learners learn best by touch—feeling something or physically performing a task. An old saying comes to mind as an example of a tactile learner: "Tell me and I'll forget. Show me and I'll remember. Help me do it and I'll understand." This group can be the most difficult to teach effectively. Having an integrated curriculum is one answer to this need. The teacher can use art, physical activity, music, and even recess to teach the tactile learner.

In my third-grade classroom I taught division to the auditory and visual learners with ease. But I discovered that I had lost my tactile learners, so I racked my brain and came up with an idea. We lined up and started out the back door of the school. On the way to the playground we stopped in the gravel, and each child picked up a number of rocks equal to the age of his or her mother. Then we marched to the tables on the playground, where I told each student to divide his or her rocks into groups equal to the child's age. Instantly, we had thirty divided by eight, twenty-eight divided by nine, and so on. It then became easy for them to see that there were leftovers.

They were rewarded with ten minutes of extra recess. When they began working in their workbooks, they had a memory to fall back on. I would say, "Your mother is eighty-five, and you are nine." They would then divide the larger number by the smaller.

Seldom will a child depend strictly on one style of learning. More often, children will use a combination, and some can learn equally well regardless of the teaching style. On the other hand, some will have trouble learning

Sweet Pickle Relish, Sunflowers, and Old Spare Tires

no matter what style. This is when it is important for the teacher to keep experimenting until something works, and then pass this information on to the next teacher.

Out of curiosity, I completed a survey and discovered that I am an equally visual-tactile learner. My older son is a visual-tactile learner, while my younger son is a visual-auditory-tactile learner.

The last approach to learning styles deals with *seven types of intelligence, or ways of knowing*, as follows:

1. Logical-mathematical intelligence: deals with inductive and deductive thinking, numbers and abstract patterns; sometimes called scientific thinking. A teacher should ask, "How can I bring in numbers, calculations, logic, order, or critical thinking skills?"

2. Verbal-linguistic intelligence: deals with words and language, both written and spoken. A teacher should ask, "How can I use the spoken or written word?"

3. Visual-spatial intelligence: relies on sense of sight and ability to visualize; includes ability to create mental images. A teacher should ask, "How can I use visual aids, visualization, and color?"

4. Bodily-kinesthetic intelligence: relates to physical movement and the wisdom of the body; uses brain's motor cortex, which controls bodily motion. A teacher should ask, "How can I involve body movement or hands-on experiences?"

5. Musical-rhythmic intelligence: deals with tonal patterns, sounds, rhythms, and beats. A teacher should ask, "How can I bring in music or environmental sounds, or set information in a rhythmic or melodic framework?"

6. Interpersonal intelligence: has to do with person-to-person relationships and communication. A teacher should ask, "How can I involve dyads (pairs) or small groups?"

7. Intrapersonal intelligence: relates to self-reflection, metacognition, awareness of internal states of being. A teacher should ask, "How can I evoke personal feelings and memories or give students choices?"

All this information can be overwhelming if it is new to you, but you can begin implementing these ideas a little at a time. As you work, a pyramid effect will develop. You will lay foundations as you work through the seven intelligences. You will find that you have taught using all three learning styles, and then you will discover that you have also covered both sides of the brain.

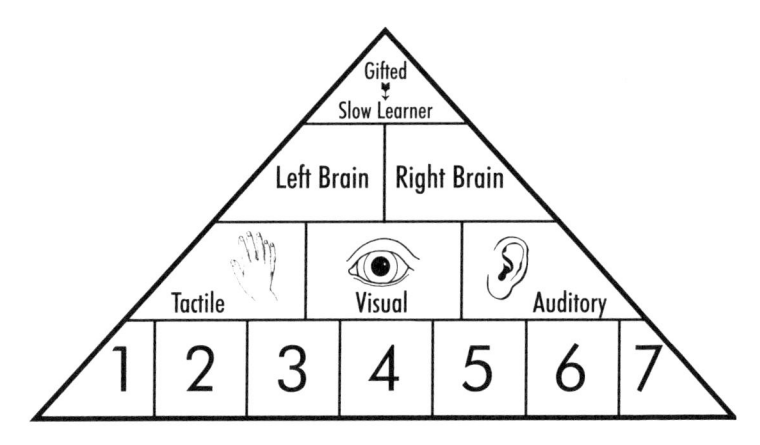

An awareness of the different learning styles will bring success to more of your students and to you as well. Few experiences in life feel as good as knowing that you have nailed down a lesson and reached every child!

Here is a poem by one of my favorite authors, Shel Silverstein, from *A Light in the Attic*, which illustrates how different people see the world differently. In short, folks are as different as sweet pickle relish, sunflowers, and old spare tires, but they all have a place.

Reflections

Each time I see the Upside-Down Man
Standing in the water,
I look at him and start to laugh,
Although I shouldn't ought ter.
For maybe in another world,
Another time,
Another town,
Maybe he is right side up,
And I am upside down.

—Shel Silverstein

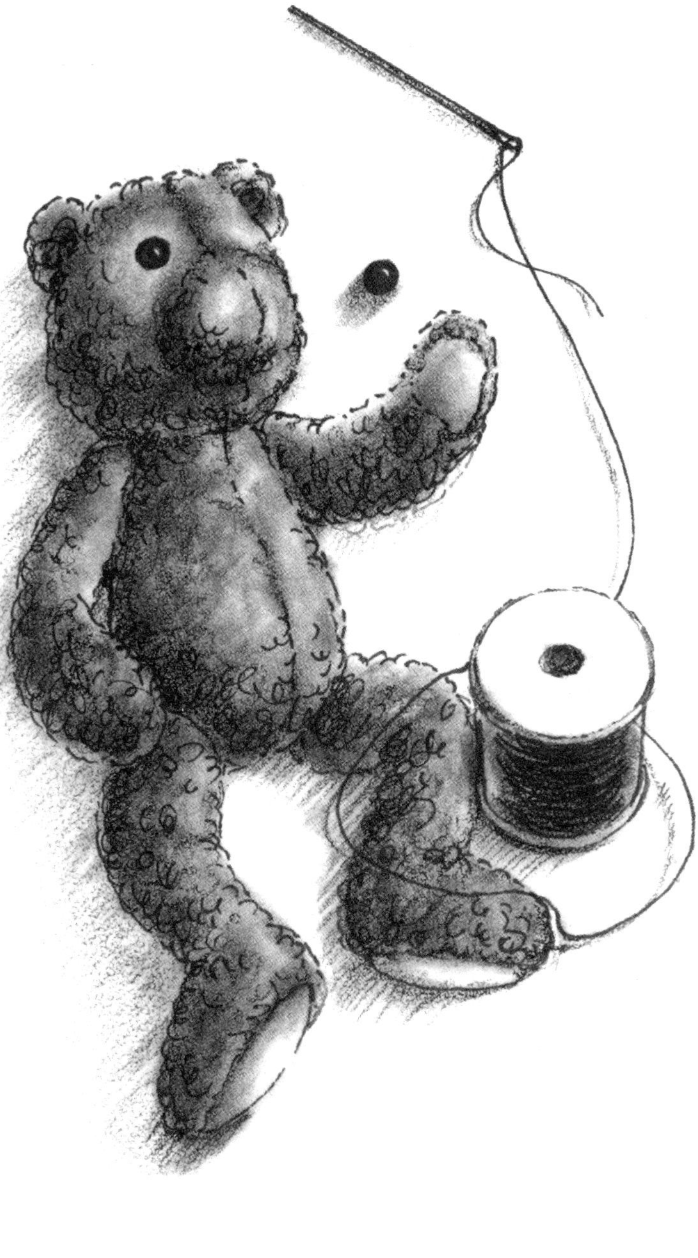

chapter four

Reach, Teach, Evaluate
(The Plan)

As a Sunday school teacher, there have been times that planning seemed to take up precious time that I could not spare. I knew the story. We could play a game and color a worksheet. After all, isn't that what Sunday school is all about? I would march into the class and begin with confidence: "Today the lesson is about David and Goliath. David killed the giant with a stone from a sling. Here is a picture of them to color. Now we will play Guess Who. I need a tall boy and a short boy. Can you guess who is David? Now, class is over. . . . *What*?! Twenty minutes! You mean I still have *forty* minutes left with these kids? What am I going to do?"

The kids sensed the desperation and became rowdy. I

started feeling frustrated. And the domino effect occurred. I left feeling that I did not care if those brats came back or not, and they left feeling that they had the grouchiest teacher in the world. In the end, I lost more than my precious time.

Planning is so vital that without it one cannot teach effectively. In this chapter we will discuss the what, why, and how of planning a lesson. Bryce B. Hudgins said:

> In the absence of planning, teaching can become confused, disorganized and chaotic, resulting in negative consequences both for the learning of pupils and for their attitudes toward the teacher and school. The teacher who can consistently provide meaningful, educational experiences without giving careful prior consideration to his goals and the means of achieving them is rare, or more likely nonexistent.

Habits and ruts are the result of not planning.

A song in 1962 entitled "Little Houses" by Malvina Reynolds describes life without planning for growth and change. It speaks of "little boxes on the hillside . . . a green one and a blue one and a yellow one, and they're all made out of ticky-tacky, and they all look just the same." Then it describes the inhabitants: they all go to the university and get put in boxes. "There's doctors and there's lawyers and there's business executives, and they're all made out of ticky-tacky, and they come out all the same." These people have children, who all go to school, summer camp, and the university. "And they all get put in boxes and they come out just the same."

People need planning in their daily lives, and likewise,

teachers need planning to provide the best opportunities for the children in their class. A teacher needs to (1) formulate and select what is most appropriate for the children to learn (objectives), (2) consider a variety of materials and approaches and select those most likely to result in the hoped-for learning (procedures), and (3) employ the best means of determining the extent to which the objectives have been attained (evaluation). With these statements in mind, let us discuss the "how" of effective planning.

First, well-defined *objectives* offer the teacher a platform on which to build a lesson that will bring about desired changes in the learner. Objectives give direction, guide the selection of experiences, help to provide balance, provide a foundation for evaluation, and provide a basis for change. An objective states the behavioral change that will take place in the student. It does not state the action to be taken by the teacher or describe the method by which the lesson will be taught. For example, instead of stating, "I will teach the children to get along," we might say, "The children will use cooperative dialogue while playing in the centers."

Once a clear objective is in place, the second step is *procedure*. It consists of the activities and methods that are used to change behavior or impart knowledge. It can be broken into three main parts: introduction, body, and closure.

The introduction lays the foundation for the whole lesson. It establishes motivation and interest. As an example, I sometimes go into a class and act upset to the point that I demand silence. Then I ask, "Do you want to know what's wrong?" The students always answer, "Yes." I then tell a story about incompetence in some imaginary situa-

TEACHING IN PERSPECTIVE

tion—about being short-changed at the store, a silly rule on the playground, or some other infraction upon my dignity or welfare. While they are still wondering where I am going, I state the purpose of the lesson and tie the need for their learning some information to the opening situation. The same can be done with world crises, role playing with children, puppets, and so on. In this way, the importance of the lesson is established at the outset. If learners can have fun with the material or see the importance of the information, they will learn it much faster and retain it longer.

Planning activities that build upon the introduction and attain the objective is important, because it is during the instruction and independent practice that the learning takes place. As we discussed in chapter 3, there are various ways to plan activities that meet each child's need, no matter what the dominant learning style. An effective teacher will provide a wide variety of activities and present the lesson for auditory, visual, and tactile learners.

Practice reinforces the teaching; it is not evaluation. (Tutoring falls under this category, and it may be necessary in some cases.) Games, role playing, small group activities, individual projects, lectures, research, computers, and much more can offer variety to the lessons.

The closure of a lesson is the wrap-up and review. Every time the lesson is stopped, there needs to be closure, even if the lesson is to continue. During the closure, the teacher may want to include evaluation. The teacher repeats the objective and purpose for the lesson, reminds the children of the reason it is important to them, and tries to end the session with a good feeling.

If a student is having trouble grasping a concept, the

teacher should offer him hope that success will come next time. For the student who feels stress, the teacher should offer calm reassurance. It is desirable to make some form of contact with each pupil at the close of every lesson. If the teacher cannot feasibly touch or talk to each one, then he or she can make eye contact and exchange expressions. Experience will help the teacher to read the eyes of the students. A caring teacher will never let a child with a puzzled look leave a class without offering an explanation or asking if he needs more. If need be, the teacher can set up one-on-one time or mentoring. The main thing is not to leave any loose ends, because if one gets pulled it can unravel an entire class.

Finally, *evaluation* is a must. To evaluate is to monitor the mastery of the objective by the student and to pinpoint assets and defects in the instruction and materials used. Testing, observing and recording, and conferencing, are types of formal evaluation. Informal evaluation may occur by simply observing for mastery, asking if there are any questions, letting the students monitor each other in small-group practice, or even playing a game.

I have taught in the public schools of Texas long enough to remember the days before formal teacher evaluations. I often attempted to become a better teacher, but it seemed that I could not find the specific need for improvement. I wish I could say that I always rated as exceptional once formal evaluations were introduced.

One time while I was being observed, a child began to get out of control with his banter. I knew that he was teasing and that disciplining him would cause him great stress. I tried repeatedly to regain control but wound up making a bad situation worse. After the sessions with my principal and lots of tears, I learned more about classroom control than I had in any other time.

Once, when an outside evaluator was in my class, I taught vigorously through my introduction and instruction. As we went into independent practice, however, one of the children piped up, "We already done that page." It was true. I had taught so much better during the formal evaluation that neither the kids nor I remembered the lesson from the day before. Obviously, I had previously just gone through the motions. I flopped on the evaluation, but I learned that I should teach every lesson at my best.

On the 1995-96 Texas Teacher Appraisal System form, there are four domains and nine criteria that are evaluated by formal observation. Here is a checklist of the evaluation:

DOMAIN I: INSTRUCTIONAL STRATEGIES

1. Provides opportunities for students to participate actively and successfully.
    a. varies activities appropriately
    b. interacts with group(s) appropriately
    c. extends responses/contributions
    d. provides time for response/consideration
    e. implements at appropriate level
2. Evaluates and provides feedback on student progress during instruction.
    a. communicates learning expectations
    b. monitors student performance
    c. solicits responses/demonstrations for assessment
    d. reinforces correct response/performances
    e. provides corrective feedback/clarifies/none needed
    f. reteaches/none needed

DOMAIN II: CLASSROOM MANAGEMENT AND ORGANIZATION

3. Organizes materials and students.
    a. secures student attention
    b. uses procedures/routines
    c. gives clear administrative directions/none needed
    d. maintains appropriate seating/group
    e. has materials/aids/facilities ready
4. Maximizes amount of time available for instruction.
    a. begins promptly/avoids waste at end
    b. implements appropriate sequence of activities
    c. maintains appropriate pace
    d. maintains focus
    e. keeps students engaged
5. Manages student behaviors.
    a. specifies expectations for behavior/none needed
    b. prevents off-task behavior/none needed
    c. redirects/stops inappropriate/disruptive behavior/none needed
    d. applies rules consistently and fairly/none needed
    e. reinforces desired behavior when appropriate

DOMAIN III: PRESENTATION OF SUBJECT MATTER

6. Teaches for cognitive, affective, and/or psychomotor learning.
    a. begins with appropriate introduction
    b. presents information in appropriate sequence
    c. relates content to prior/future learning
    d. defines/describes concepts: skills, attitudes, interests
    e. elaborates critical attributes
    f. stresses generalization/principle/rule

7. Uses effective communication skills.
   a. makes no significant errors
   b. explains content/task(s) clearly
   c. stresses important points/dimensions
   d. uses correct grammar
   e. uses accurate language
   f. demonstrates written skill

DOMAIN IV: LEARNING ENVIRONMENT

8. Uses strategies to motivate students for learning.
   a. relates content to interest/experiences
   b. emphasizes values/importance of activity/content
   c. reinforces/praises efforts
   d. challenges students
9. Maintains supportive environment.
   a. avoids sarcasm/negative criticism
   b. establishes climate of courtesy
   c. encourages slow/reluctant students
   d. establishes and maintains positive rapport

SUGGESTIONS / COMMENTS:

This evaluation is lengthy and formal, but with enough practice and patience, you can become a model teacher by choosing one domain, working to master it in your teaching, and then moving on to another. Soon these things will become habit.

Most discipline problems that occur are a direct result of the teacher's planning or, rather, lack of planning. Planning is vital to teaching.

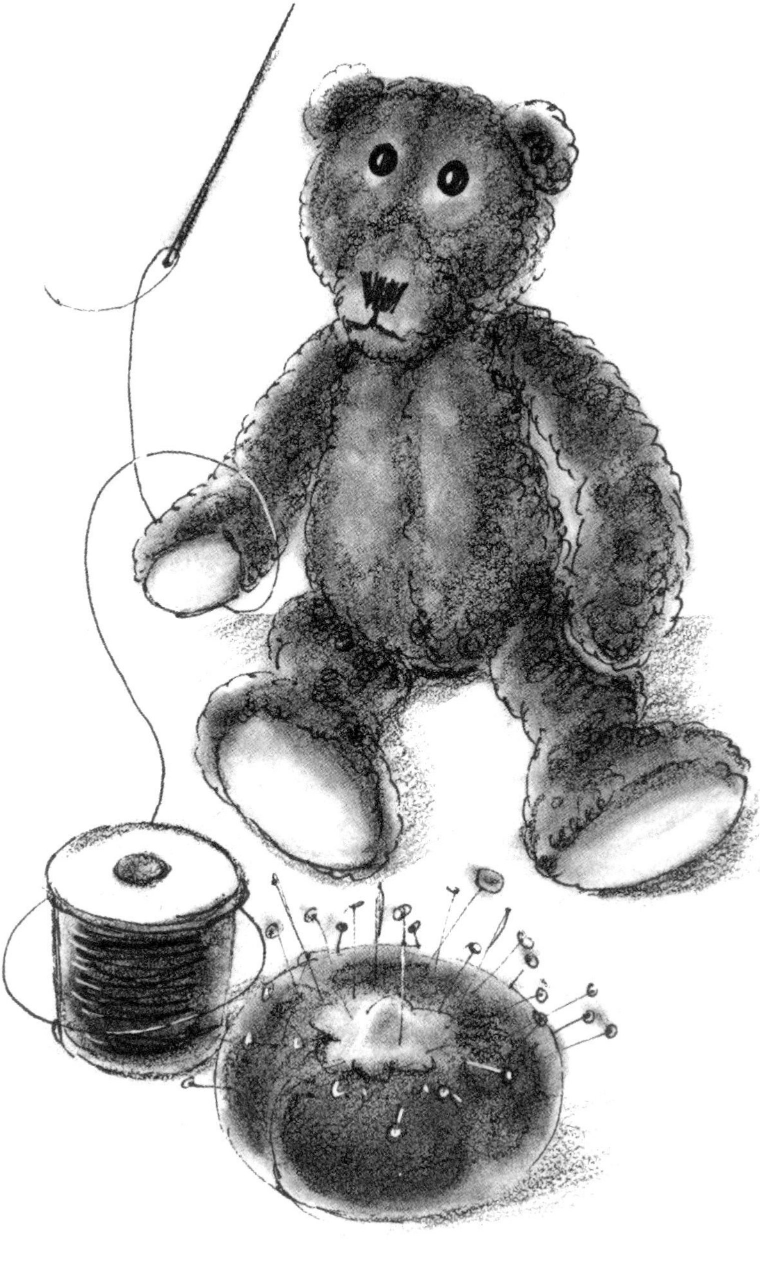

chapter five

Classroom Discipline

"Hi, Amy," Ms. Lou greeted the sweet, never-do-anything-wrong child who sat near her desk. Automatically she shifted her eyes to the opposite side of the room to Donald's desk. Sure enough, he was out of his seat, and a loud discussion was going on in his area. "Donald, did you take your medicine?" Her voice was raised and so was her finger as she pointed to the door.

"No, ma'am. I can't, 'cause Mama didn't have the money to buy it this month."

"Ohhh," the teacher groaned as a look of frustration swept over her face. "Well, just sit down and be quiet."

The other students began to chime in.

"Yeah!"

TEACHING IN PERSPECTIVE

"Tell your mama that you need your pills."
"I think you need a fist in your nose."
"Now, he's gonna mess up our Friday party."

Finally, in an attempt to regain her class, Ms. Lou called out, "Okay, class, time to open your books. Class. Class! CLASS!"

This is often the story of Donald's morning. You see, he has attention deficit hyperactivity disorder (ADHD) and comes from a single-parent family where his mom is struggling to provide for two other children. He is from a poor section of town, and his only close friend is his dog. He is bright, athletic, and very artistic. He has taught himself several gymnastic tumbles that can impress a crowd. However, ADHD keeps his self-esteem so low that he feels he must struggle constantly to be accepted.

I'll never forget the day I saw Donald's stop sign. I entered his class to teach art and was going about my instruction when Don met my eye and announced, "I took two pills this morning." Since one of my own sons is on medication because of ADD (attention deficit disorder), I immediately tuned in to him. "Is that what your doctor prescribed for you to take?" I questioned.

His response was shattering as he said, "No, but everybody hates me when I don't take it, so I have been taking two."

"Does your mother know?"

"No, ma'am."

"Donald, not *everybody* hates you. Are you seriously taking two?"

"Yep, and they do hate me. You even hate me." He said it so matter-of-factly that I was taken back.

"No, I don't."

Classroom Discipline

"Yes, you do, when I don't have my medicine."

Realizing that I had to do something, I sent Donald out into the hall, telling him that he was not in trouble but that we needed to talk. After engaging the rest of the class in a drawing assignment, I went to Donald and closed the door behind me. I knew how he was feeling, and this was a delicate moment. What I would say could make or break this child that was reaching out to me.

"Donald," I began, "how long has it been since someone gave you a great big hug and said, 'I love you'"?

"A long time . . . a real long time." He dropped his head and looked so sad.

"Well, Donald, I do love you," I said as my arms took him in. "I really do."

He wrapped his arms around my middle and squeezed me; then he started patting me on the back. He was soaking up the love and affection. After several seconds of this cherished embrace we stepped back. Both of us had tears in our eyes, but Donald had a smile a mile wide. We went back to class, and he began his art assignment.

I could not get him off of my mind, and I knew that he needed more. The next morning I asked him what his favorite food was. At lunch I picked him up with a bag in my hand from the local hamburger restaurant. We went to the cafeteria where we sat at the teacher table and had cheeseburgers, curly fries, and even a glass of tea. No kids drink tea in the cafeteria in elementary school.

We talked. We laughed. We shared. I told him about my son and about me when I was a little girl, a time when ADD was unheard of. Then I told him about a fuzzy puppy that got burrs in his fur. When the puppy would jump in Donald's lap he would push the pup away because the burrs hurt. The puppy felt lonely and did not understand. He did not want a bath or to be brushed, but when he was all cleaned up Donald could love on him once again. At last I leaned close, caught his hand, and said, "Donald, when you don't have your medicine you have trouble controlling your behavior, and that is like having burrs in your fur. The teachers and other students have a hard time being nice to you. And just as the puppy had to have a bath, you must allow us to help take care of the burrs so that we can show you how we really feel about you."

Now, when I notice unacceptable behavior in Donald I say, "Remember the burrs." Things seem to be going better for him.

The term *discipline* covers a broad subject. It reminds us of the word *disciple*—a follower who learns from the actions of a leader. A good leader makes good disciples. And good disciples learn effective discipline. The aim of discipline is to develop self-control within the pupil. Discipline is an intellectual matter, never blind conformity and enforced routine.

Knowing the causes of behavior and controlling the causes are two vital elements to effective classroom discipline. There are basic needs and urges within all human beings that bring about actions. When the actions bring satisfaction to oneself and others because of the furtherance of a worthy purpose, then the results are desirable. When the needs and urges are interrupted, the frustrated actions are undesirable. Needs are present not only in children but also in all of us. We can categorize them as the needs for security, social recognition and approval, success, activity, and integration.

By setting up a classroom and giving specific atten-

Classroom Discipline

tion to the needs of children and their developmental stages, we will invariably need to maintain a consistent set of rules. Very early in my own sons' lives I would have them recite the three reasons for rules, so that they could see why I enforced them. They would hold up three stubby fingers and recite, "One: for safety of me and others. Two: for protection of property. Three: to help me be a better person." A few times I had to back down on my rules after giving consideration to all of these. Once they were playing loudly in their room and I had to consider, Are they hurting anyone? Are they tearing up anything? Will it make them be bad people? No. So, I went to another room to work, and let them play.

It is important for a child to realize that every action results in a consequence. It is also important to give children the opportunity to make decisions and reap the consequences.

It is good, when possible, to allow the children to set the rules and consequences of their environment. They will usually be firmer and more demanding than the teacher would be. Then the teacher can remind the students, "But you made the rules." In all cases, the teacher must be consistent and must make sure that all students understand what is expected of them.

Consequences can be either positive or negative. Positive consequences will bring satisfaction and pleasant emotions. Negative consequences will cause dissatisfaction and unpleasant emotions.

Two different people may view the same consequence differently. For this reason, the teacher must be certain that she knows her students. For instance, my older son works better in isolation. As a reward for his sharing on

TEACHING IN PERSPECTIVE

the playground the teacher could let him work in the isolation space. My younger son is a lover of groups and hates to be alone; therefore as punishment the same teacher may send him to the isolation space for not sharing.

Negative consequences are often called punishment. It is extremely important that the punishment fit the crime. Excessive punishment becomes torture. A kindergartner who sits incorrectly in his chair may need to sit in his chair for five or ten minutes. Demanding more would be overdoing it. On the other hand, a fifth grader who throws food in the cafeteria would need a much more severe action.

It is important for the teacher to think about what she is saying to a pupil when discussing a disciplinary situation. The purpose is to build self-control within the individual, not merely to force conformity to the rules. The teacher needs to help students understand why and how they can reach this goal. A poor choice of words or how words are said can cause wounds in the mind and emotions of children that never heal. I have heard verbal torture in the form of sarcasm, demeaning slurs, and excessive volume.

Know your own limitations and the limitations of the situation you are in. Beware of idle threats. A teacher should never punish a child to get even with him or because of a dislike for him. It is your job and responsibility to bring every child to his fullest potential while he is in your care.

Punishment and scolding can come in a variety of ways—verbal, physical, and nonverbal. Verbal punishment involves speaking directly to the child or class. Nonverbal punishment could be a simple frown during eye contact or another nonverbal expression of displeasure. Physical punishment occurs when a child feels the punishment on his or her body. A growing concern for child abuse has caused every action of teachers to be closely monitored, so they must remain well within the limits of their role, never hitting or spanking a student. When they do administer some type of punishment, they should document the incident in writing with the date.

Documentation in Sunday school and other volunteer situations can be a lifeline for a teacher. For instance, a child named Joe consistently caused disruptions. He talked to his friends during lessons and made rude comments to the teachers. I invited him out of class, where we discussed his behavior and potential consequences. As soon as church was over, I went to his mother and related the events. I made her aware not only of his behavior but of his response and how I handled him. She found out that he had been informed of the consequences, thus letting her know them also. At the close of the conference I told her that we could work together on his behavior and reassured her that if there was any more trouble she would be the first to know. This conversation served as an informal verbal documentation. However, it is still a good idea to write everything down.

Positive consequences are often called rewards. Once again, the reward should fit the action. A verbal "thank you" is enough reward for someone who opens a door for another. However, if a child stays late and staples papers for the whole class, it would be appropriate to buy him a soda, or perhaps pizza.

Verbal praise is one of the best rewards. Many kids light up when a teacher takes time to notice that they did a good job. Physical rewards such as a hug, pat, high five, and so on are also inexpensive and fulfilling. A word of caution: physical rewards must be well within the safety zone and limited to what is clearly appropriate, since teachers are in the eye of the public all the time.

Nonverbal rewards are resources that I apply liberally. Smiles can cover miles. A wink, nod, thumbs up, okay sign, and so on are great for making children know how good they are. Tangible rewards are rewards that they can hold or receive in some way. These are great for rewarding a child upon the completion of a job. The teacher can set a goal, name the prize, and then help the student work for it.

I often give all of these rewards in one setting. Donald, from the beginning of this chapter, was a classic example. Together we set goals for him. Then when he attained a goal, there were cheers (verbal), hugs and high fives (physical), smiles (nonverbal), and a token toy (tangible).

Praise and rewards that bring satisfaction are incredibly positive motivators, while punishment and rewards that do not bring satisfaction can work against the objective of self-discipline. Children have a natural, built-in desire to please the adults and peers around them. We have the overwhelming ability to destroy this desire with our actions in reaction to them. From the earliest awareness of their surroundings, they mimic and show pleasure when adults are pleased with them.

I distinctly remember the people in my life who took time to see me, hear me, and count me worthy to listen to. It was important to me when Dad showed approval at my kindergarten graduation. I had the same feeling of doing something right for him as I graduated from eighth grade, high school, and college with a bachelor's degree, and it was no less with my master's degree and the birth of my sons.

On the other hand, consistent negative reinforcement can create barriers and handicaps that are difficult to overcome. My fourth-grade teacher planted a seed of self-doubt that grew until I was in summer school between the ninth and tenth grades. It was that summer that Dad sat me down, as a fourteen-year-old skinny little girl, and told me that he wanted to go to Alpine, Texas, to start a mission work. He said that he would need my help and he was counting on me to act like the example of what we wanted the people of our church to be. Upon entering my sophomore year my grades climbed to A's and B's again. My appearance changed to that of a lady. Under Mother's guidance and instruction, I started helping in the local children's church with a puppet ministry. My parents helped me begin my career with children by believing in me. That is really what kids want to know and feel—that we really and truly believe in them.

I try to talk to my students who are causing problems and find out why. So many times, they believe that the world of kids and the world of adults are too far apart for them to reach across the span. As adults, we often have to cross back over to them to help them across. Donald was a classic example. Yes, he broke the rules, and yes, he had to be punished, but after we talked he understood that he was still a great person and that I knew he was.

Another time, a very defiant fifth-grade boy stood up and began to defy everything I said and did. I promptly separated him from the group, and in the privacy of the hall I cornered him against the wall and demanded, "What have I done to you? Why are you treating me this way? Have I ever hurt you in any way? What are you trying to prove to me?" When I finished he had no answers, so I lowered my voice and explained to him that my feelings were hurt and that his action had forced me to be unpleasant to him, which I hated to do. I then pointed out that the other students were not impressed with his behavior and that he was keeping them from learning, so if he wanted to continue to be in my class he would conform or suffer more severe consequences. He felt (1) ashamed of himself, (2) understanding from me and where I was coming from, (3) compassion from me, (4) dissatisfaction with the results of his actions, (5) that I believed in him, and (6) that he had another chance.

My first day of my first-grade class was underway when a kindergarten teacher told me about a child who had called her a racial slur and spent a great deal of time under a table last year. The little girl was in my class. Before the week was out, sure enough she exploded in class. I immediately came to her desk and said sternly, "Kanella, go to the hall!" The other students instantly froze in place to see what would happen next, because they remembered last year.

I followed close behind her, and when we were out I shut the door firmly (well, okay, I slammed it) before I demanded, "Kanella, look at me. Look at me, girl. Look into my eyes. Do you believe I love you?" She was so startled that I softened my voice and asked her again. Openly she gave her honest answer, "Naw." She had never felt that a white woman could love or believe in a black girl. I told her with a hug that I knew she was smart, that she could act like a big girl, that I did love her, and most of all, that I wanted to be her friend, too. We hugged, and Kanella's classroom behavior made a turnaround. She is grown now, and I am still getting hugs from her.

I could tell of case after case in which the only discipline children needed was for me to let them know that I cared. Most children know how to act; they just need prompting and patience.

Becoming a mentor or involving mentors in the classroom is a positive way to establish confidence and self-discipline. Nonworking parents, retired grandparents, and preachers are excellent resources for mentors. Mentors can give rewards, monitor weekly progress reports, remember holidays, and generally make a child feel super. Older children make great mentors for younger children, and they in turn benefit also.

Fairness should be a goal of every teacher. I received the greatest compliment of my life when a grandmother told me that her grandson had said, "The thing I like about Ms. Magic is that she is fair." I strive to treat all children fairly regardless of sex, color, or creed. If a child walks up and wants to talk to me but I am involved in conversation with an adult, I will often have the adult wait while the child has my attention. It only takes a minute, but the child feels that I believe in and care about him.

B's in Discipline
Be sure; be firm;
Be as brief as possible.
Be kind; be patient;
Believe in the child.
Be consistent; be fair.
—Avis McMullen

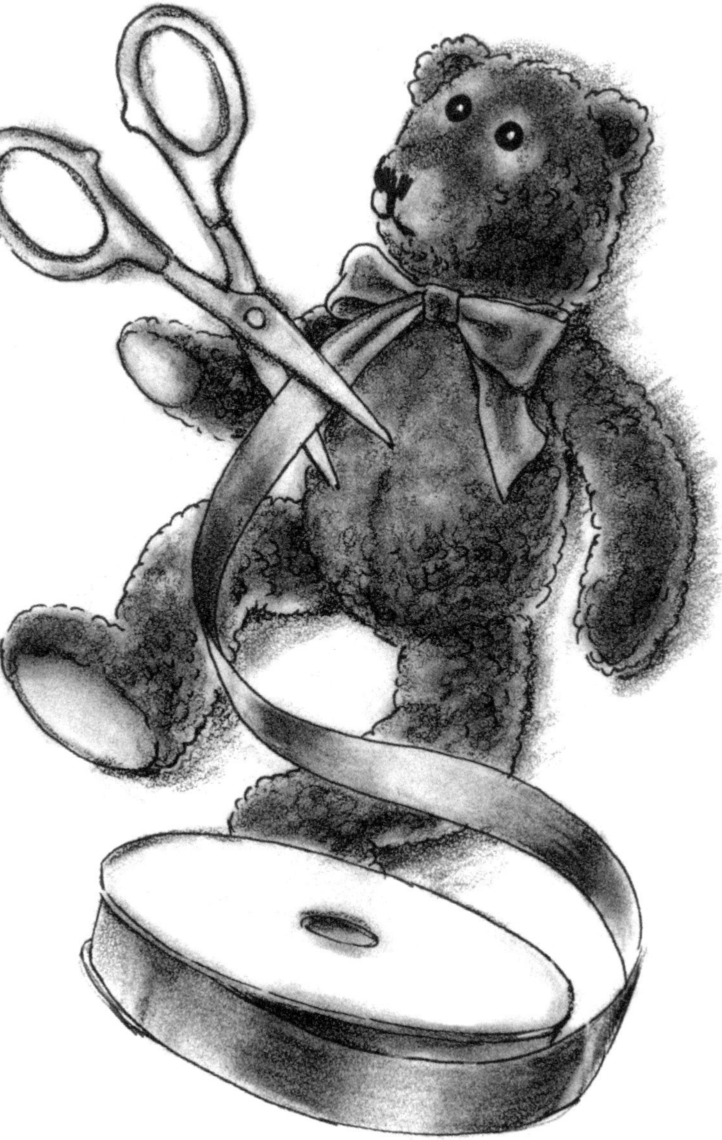

chapter six

Just Legal Matters

Who Ordered the Broiled Face?
>Well, here you are,
>Just as you ordered,
>Broiled face with butter sauce,
>Mashed potatoes on the side.
>What do you mean you wanted it fried?
>>—Shel Silverstein

Not every person wants teachers to succeed. Some people wait for a chance to serve the teacher's face fried, broiled, or smashed. In many cases, the reason is that at some time they have encountered a teacher who entered a classroom for the wrong reasons or lost focus once there. Some teachers make bad choices, and we have to protect children in every possible way from them.

Sometimes teachers act inappropriately by accident or because of a lack of knowledge. The law states certain requirements when dealing with children, and it is important for teachers to learn them. It is good to attend a workshop or take a class on this topic. We cannot cover the entire spectrum of legal issues, but let us briefly discuss some of the more common causes of lawsuits involving teachers.

The issue of child abuse and exploitation is quickly growing more and more important. Teachers should personally know their students and understand their perception of certain situations. Parents become concerned when children are embarrassed in front of their peers, publicly humiliated, punished excessively, or touched in a questionable way (some hugging, patting, and caressing).

Teachers must constantly assess the situation. They should be alert to comments and keep the parents informed of any questionable incident. They should carefully document problems and keep clear records, including dates, names, times, and descriptive notes. They can never cover too many bases. Frequent parent conferences and good parental relationships are essential. Children sometimes relate incidents or statements inaccurately or with a different connotation than the teacher intended. In such cases, the proof falls on the teacher, so she must be prepared.

Confidential information and records must be kept confidential. Never be found guilty of discussing records or situations that are confidential with anyone who is not directly related to the situation or who does not need the information. Unverified statements that damage someone's reputation can be slander when spoken and libel

Just Legal Matters

when written, and both can result in legal liability. Even when the information is demonstrably true, sharing damaging information publicly or to someone who does not need to know can be invasion of privacy, which can result in legal penalties.

Sometimes confidential information needs to be discussed, such as health records, learning information, and behaviors. However, the teacher must be sure that she is disclosing the information for the good of the child and to an appropriate person.

One day I was dealing with a rather unruly child in my art class and decided to follow my discipline plan to the finish. One of the final steps was to use a paddle, which is allowed in public schools in Texas. Fortunately, I took him to his homeroom teacher for her to witness. I had the paddle raised when the teacher and I made eye contact over his head. She mouthed, "Don't hit him." I was puzzled but lowered the paddle and asked her to step aside and explain why. She then related that she had just been told that he had a pacemaker and a sudden blow could kill him. I almost had a heart attack! I scolded him firmly, made empty threats about the next time he acted up, sent him back in the classroom, and then wilted. Needless to say, shortly after that my discipline plan underwent a major overhaul. Communication with parents and administration is important.

Sometimes a teacher may need to search a child's belongings for something, but in doing so she must take great caution not to invade the privacy of the individual. If a teacher needs to search a certain child's things, it is better to inspect the belongings of all the children, searching the suspected child neither first nor last. The laws about search and seizure are pretty rigid.

In a third-grade class, a certain boy wrote profanity on notes and dropped them around the room. One of the other students told me that he had more such notes in his desk. I searched all the desks on his row and the rows on each side. Later in the week, I found myself in the principal's office facing questions from his parents. I was glad that I could honestly say that I had performed a random search.

Another note of caution: Never, for any reason, put your hand into a child's pocket to search it. Ask the child to empty the pocket and turn it inside out for you.

Last, the law is clear that if you suspect child abuse and do not report it, you can be held liable for the damages. Never hesitate to refer a child that you even slightly suspect may have been abused. You may be the child's only hope of getting help.

One day, Heather called me into the girls' restroom to see what was hurting her back. What I saw still sends chills down my spine. There were scars that had healed over, fresh scars still healing, old sores, and some very recent scabs from where she had been beaten with an extension cord. After I reported the incident, her single mother was able to take some parent training and get the help she needed for her life. The story had a happy ending.

Make sure you understand the procedure that your school or church has adopted for situations such as this, and report them to the proper person in authority. Find out the number of your state's toll-free child abuse hotline in case you are the one who needs to call. Your action could mean the salvation of a child's life. It would be better to sound a false alarm than to read about one of your kids in the hospital report or, worse, the obituary section.

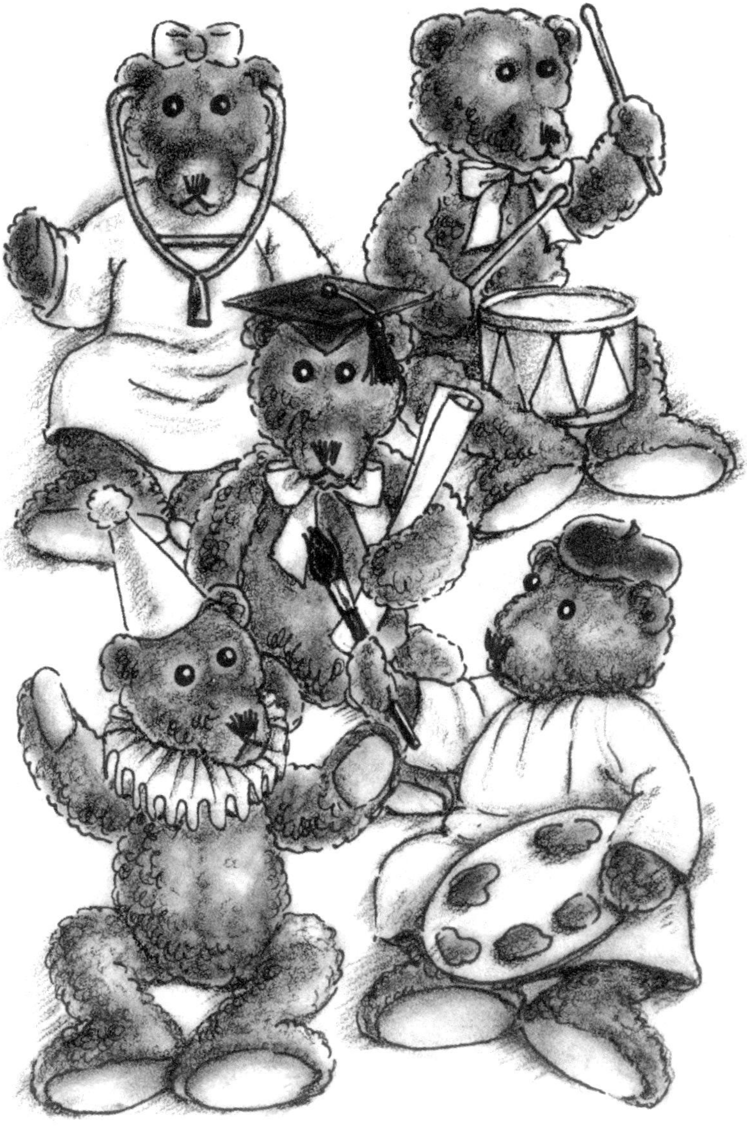

chapter seven

Wit, Wisdom, and Whatnots

"Whoso loveth instruction loveth knowledge: but he that hateth reproof is brutish" (Proverbs 12:1).

Great teachers with a mighty message promote positive learning.

Teaching children to count is not as important as teaching them what counts.

Far away in the sunshine are my highest aspirations. I may not reach them but I can look up and see their beauty, believe in them, and try to follow where they lead. (Mary Alcott)

TEACHING IN PERSPECTIVE

What I can think about I can talk about. What I can say I can write. What I can write I can read. I can read what I write and what other people can write for me to read. (Roach Van Allen)

A teacher is
Someone who is wise,
Who cares about the students
And wears no disguise;
But is honest and open,
And shares from the heart,
Not just lessons from books,
But life where you are.
A teacher takes time
To help and tutor
With English or math
Or on a computer.
It's someone who's patient,
Even in stress;
Who never gives less
Than the very best.

—Rebecca Barlow Jordan

Always laugh when you can; it is a cheap medicine.

Life is a test. It is only a test. If this were your actual life, you would have been given better instructions.

A teacher is someone who knows all of the answers, but only when she asks the questions.

"Let your gentleness be evident to all. The Lord is near" (Philippians 4:5, NIV).

You're in the building business. Build self-esteem in yourself and others!

"She openeth her mouth with wisdom; and in her tongue is the law of kindness" (Proverbs 31:26).

A Teacher's Prayer

Lord, please help me to spread a banquet of knowledge before my students. Help me to encourage them to feed themselves with healthy, nourishing knowledge that will strengthen their minds. Help me not to spoon-feed them, starve them, or give them bland, unappetizing fare. Give them an appetite for learning good things. Amen.

Teacher

Teachers work so hard at teaching
That we sometimes quite forget
That they have a home and family
And needs that must be met.
But we're giving you this gift to say
We know and we care—
We appreciate your faithfulness
And wisdom that you share.
May God bless you in the classroom;
May He bless you in the home;
May He comfort, guide, and strengthen you
Wherever you may roam.

TEACHING IN PERSPECTIVE

Mothers and teachers of children fill places so great that there isn't an angel in heaven that wouldn't be glad to give a bushel of diamonds to come down here and take their place. (Billy Sunday)

A Teacher's Prayer

God grant me wisdom, creativity, and love.

With wisdom, I may look to the future and see the effect that my teaching will have on these children, and thus adapt my methods to fit the needs of each one.

With creativity, I can prepare new and interesting projects that can challenge my students and expand their minds to set higher goals and dream loftier dreams.

With love, I can praise my students for jobs well done and encourage them to get up and go when they fail.

Lord, reveal Yourself through me.

Amen.

God never imposes a duty without giving time and strength to perform it.

Reading is actually an adventure; it's like a journey to a new place. (Charles Schulz)

Busy kids are happy kids.

Education is knowing what you want, knowing where to get it, and knowing what to do with it after you get it.

To know is nothing at all, to imagine is everything. (A. France)

In the Middle of a Bad Day

Father,
Help me to recognize a bad day for what it is—A DAY.
It does not represent the rest of the year,
or the rest of the month,
or even the rest of the week.
Keep me from making value judgments based
on this day.
Keep me from deciding that the children are hopeless,
that my work is in vain,
and that I am a failure.

Oh, Father,
I'm discouraged and tired today,
But I'm not a failure.
I'm disorganized and frazzled today,
But the classroom still functions.
I'm impatient and crabby today,
But the children know that I love them.

It's a bad day today,
but it's only a day.
It will pass.
Give me the patience to wait it out
And to hold my letter of resignation until tomorrow!

It's good to have money and the things that money can buy, but it's good, too, to check up once in a while and make sure you haven't lost the things money can't buy.

Out of the mouths of babes often come remarks their parents should never have said in the first place.

TEACHING IN PERSPECTIVE

Cracklings

As our children grow and learn, they fall down. We are quick to set them back up as long as they stay on the table of education. However, a few fall to the rug of remediation. Will we take the time to set them back up on the table? Or will we gently nudge them out of our way? When the fallen ones are off the rug, the broom of circumstance will sweep them into the cracks of life to be trampled by the feet of society. This is the making of "cracklings" in the fast-paced, self-centered lifestyle that we live in.

I pray for a teacher who will help my children to stay on the table.

—Avis McMullen

The little child digs his well in the seashore sand and the great Atlantic, miles deep, miles wide, is stirred all through and through to fill it for him.

September is when millions of bright, shining, happy, laughing faces turn toward school. They belong to mothers.

The smartest advice on raising children is to enjoy them while they are still on your side.

Life begins as a quest of a child for the man and ends as a journey by the man to rediscover the child. (Laurens van der Post)

Wisdom is nothing more than common sense refined by learning and experience.

1915 Rules for Teachers

1. You will not marry during the term of your contract.

2. You are not to keep company with men.

3. You must be home between the hours of 8 P.M. and 6 A.M. unless attending a school function.

4. You may not loiter downtown in ice cream stores.

5. You may not travel beyond the city limits unless you have permission of the chairman of the board.

6. You may not ride in a carriage or automobile with any man unless he is your father or brother.

7. You may not smoke cigarettes.

8. You may not dress in bright colors.

9. You may under no circumstances dye your hair.

10. You must wear at least two petticoats.

11. Your dress must not be any shorter than two inches above the ankle.

12. To keep the school room neat and clean, you must: sweep the floor at least once daily, scrub the floor at least once a week with hot, soapy water, clean the blackboards at least once a day, and start the fire at 7 A.M. so the room will be warm by 8 A.M.

If you won't believe what he comes to school and tells you, I won't believe what he comes home and tells me.

Mondays make Fridays look even better.

Looking up will lift you up.

There is nothing like the glow of a child's delight to warm a teacher's heart.

Success

To laugh often and much;
To win the respect of intelligent people and affection of children;
To earn the appreciation of honest critics and endure the betrayal of false friends;
To appreciate beauty, to find the best in others;
To leave the world a bit better, whether by a healthy child, a garden patch or a redeemed social condition;
To know even one life has breathed easier because you have lived.
This is to have succeeded.

—Ralph Waldo Emerson

When in charge . . . ponder;
When in trouble . . . delegate;
When in doubt . . . mumble.

My Motto

I won't criticize it until I can improve it.
I won't put it down until I can compliment it.
I won't dislike it until I understand it.
I will give everyone a fair chance.

—Avis McMullen

It is entirely possible to know more than you understand.

The heart has reasons that reason does not understand. (J. Bossuet)

Every child who comes into the world presents a new

possibility for lifting the destiny of the human race. (Anna B. Mow)

A child is a person who is going to carry on what you have started. He is going to sit where you are sitting, and when you are gone, tend to those things which you think are important. You may adopt all the policies you please, but how they are carried out depends on him. He will assume control of your cities, states, and nations. He is going to move in and take over your churches, schools, universities, and corporations . . . the fate of humanity is in his hands. (Abraham Lincoln)

Kids Who Are Different
Here's to the kids who are different,
The kids who don't always get A's,
The kids who have ears twice the size of their peers
and noses that go on for days.
Here's to the kids who are different,
The kids they call crazy or dumb,
The kids who don't fit, with the guts and the grit,
Who dance to a different drum.
Here's to the kids who are different,
The kids with the mischievous streak,
For when they have grown, as history's shown,
It's their difference that makes them unique. What lies behind us and what lies before us are tiny matters compared to what lies within us.

We are wise to give ourselves the things we can never lose.

TEACHING IN PERSPECTIVE

Children are today's investment and tomorrow's dividend.

Whatever you wear on your heart you wear on your face. (Ima Kilgore)

Good teaching comes not from behind the desk but from behind the heart. (Elizabeth Andrew)

Never part without loving words. They might be your last.

Note: For quotes that are not attributed to someone, the author is unknown.

Bibliography

Ambron, Sueann Robins. *Child Development*. New York: Holt, Rinehart and Winston, 1978.

Collier, Calhoun C., W. Robert Houston, Robert R. Schmatz, and William J. Walsh. *Modern Elementary Education: Teaching and Learning*. New York: Macmillan Publishing Co., 1976.

Evans, Eva Knox. *All about Us*. Irvington-on-Hudson, New York: Capitol Publishing Co., 1947.

Fischer, Louis, David Schimmel, and Cynthia Kelly. *Teachers and the Law*. New York: Longman, 1987.

Hockett, John A., and E. W. Jacobsen. *Modern Practices in the Elementary School*. New York: Ginn and Company. 1938.

Silverstein, Shel. *A Light in the Attic*. New York: Harper and Row Publishers, 1981.

Wolfgang, Charles H., and Carl D. Glickman. *Solving Discipline Problems*. Boston, Mass: Allyn and Bacon, 1986.

Note: Miscellaneous items, such as the quotes from unknown authors in Chapter 7, came from various workshops, classes, friends, and family members.